Illustrated Classics From India

Stories of Shiva

The Puranas are full of legends about the victories of Shiva over the forces of evil. This volume of Amar Chitra Katha narrates five stories related to the powerful Lord Shiva.

In the first story, Brahma and Vishnu are keen to see the ascetic Shiva married. They appeal to Goddess Uma to become Shiva's consort and she is thus born to Brahma's son Daksha. She is named Sati. With severe penances, young Sati wins the love of Shiva and they marry. Later, when Daksha insults Shiva, the ever-dutiful Sati immolates herself as she wishes to be reborn to a father she can respect. True to her word. Sati is reborn as Parvati in second story of this volume. Parvati fervently woos Shiva with charm, penance and servitude, in turn. Eventually, Parvati is united with her beloved Shiva, never to be separated from him again.

The third title in this volume contains three stories of Siva. The first 'Shiva and Arjuna', is based on an episode from the Mahabharata. The tale 'Shiva the Fisherman' is told in the Tamil classic, Tiruvachagam. In 'Shiva and Markandeya', taken from the Skanda Purana, Markandeya achieves immortality by the grace of Siva. The last two volumes are dedicated to the sons of the almighty Shiva: Ganesha and Karttikeya. The first story is based on the Shiva Purana. On the heights of Mount Kailasa, the divine household of Shiva and Parvati stood divided. Out that divine dissension was born Ganesha, who rose to become perhaps the most lovable deity in the Hindu pantheon. Karttikeya, the commander-in-chief of the celestial army, is also known as Subrahmanya, Skanda, Guha and Kumara. In the southern states of India, Subrahmanya is a popular deity even today. If Parvati created Ganesha, Karettikeya was the creation of Shiva, nurtured by Agni, Ganga and the Krittikas, each in turn.

Editor: Anant Pai

Title	Script	Illustrations
Sati and Shiva	*Kamala Chandrakant*	*P. B. Kavadi*
Shiva Parvati	*Kamala Chandrakant*	*Ram Waeerkar*
Tales of Shiva	*Subba Rao*	*C. M. Vitankar*
Ganesha	*Kamala Chandrakant*	*C. M. Vitankar*
Karttikeya	*Pradip Bhattacharya & Meera Ugra*	*C. M. Vitankar*

NO. 1008 • RS. 195

INDIA BOOK HOUSE PVT. LTD.

© India Book House Pvt. Ltd. 1998   Reprinted: July 2007 ISBN: 81-7508-193-7
Published and Printed by India Book House Pvt Ltd, Mahalaxmi Chambers,
5th Floor, 22 Bhulabhai Desai Road, Mumbai 400 026, India.

SATI AND SHIVA

BRAHMA WANTED THE ASCETIC SHIVA TO GET MARRIED. VISHNU ADVISED HIM TO SERVE THE GODDESS UMA, BEG HER TO TAKE BIRTH ON EARTH, AND BECOME SHIVA'S CONSORT.

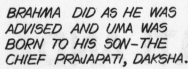

BRAHMA DID AS HE WAS ADVISED AND UMA WAS BORN TO HIS SON—THE CHIEF PRAJAPATI, DAKSHA.

SHE SHALL BE CALLED SATI.

EVEN AS A YOUNG GIRL, SATI WAS A STAUNCH DEVOTEE OF SHIVA.

WHERE IS SATI?

THERE. BUSY AS USUAL SINGING SONGS IN PRAISE OF LORD SHIVA.

SATI SOON GREW UP.

HOW BEAUTIFUL OUR DAUGHTER IS. SHE SHOULD BE GIVEN IN MARRIAGE TO ONE WHO IS HER EQUAL.

ONLY THE WORTHIEST ONE IN ALL THE THREE WORLDS SHALL BECOME HER HUSBAND.

A FEW DAYS LATER, BRAHMA AND THE SAGE NARADA CAME TO VISIT DAKSHA.

MY CHILD, PAY OBEISANCE TO THE REVERED ONES.

MAY THE MIGHTY SHIVA, WHOM YOU ADORE, BE YOUR LORD. HE HAS NOT TAKEN AND WILL NEVER TAKE ANOTHER CONSORT.

I SHALL PERFORM SEVERE PENANCES AND WIN MY LORD.

SHE BEGAN BY FASTING AND CHANTING SACRED MANTRAS.

THEN, IN DRIPPING WET CLOTHES, SHE WORSHIPPED HIM ON THE BANK OF A RIVER.

MY LORD, COME TO ME AND FULFIL MY DESTINY.

HER WHOLE BEING WAS CONCENTRATED ON SHIVA. SHE KNEW NOTHING ELSE.

3

MEANWHILE IN HEAVEN—

SATI HAS BEGUN HER PENANCES TO WIN SHIVA.

LET US GO AND BLESS HER.

SO BRAHMA AND HIS CONSORT SARASWATI, VISHNU AND HIS CONSORT LAKSHMI, AND THE CELESTIAL SAGES CAME TO SATI. BUT—

SHE IS OBLIVIOUS TO US. SO DEEP IS HER CONCENTRATION. IT IS DIVINE.

THEY WHO HAD COME TO BLESS HER SOUGHT HER BLESSINGS, INSTEAD.

THEN THEY WENT TO SHIVA.

O SHIVA, YOU TOO ACCEPT A LOVING WOMAN FOR AN ETERNAL COMPANION AS VISHNU HAS TAKEN LAKSHMI, AND I, SARASWATI.

SHIVA SMILED AND WAS QUIET FOR SOME TIME. THEN—

I AM WILLING TO MARRY. BUT I AM AN ASCETIC.

IS THERE A WOMAN WHO WILL BE A YOGINI WHEN I PRACTISE YOGA AND A LOVING HOUSE-WIFE WHEN I AM A HOUSEHOLDER?

BRAHMA WAS DELIGHTED.

O SHIVA, SATI, MY GRAND-DAUGHTER IS ONE SUCH.

YES SHIVA, SHE IS!

WHERE IS SHE?

AT THIS MOMENT SHE IS ENGAGED IN SEVERE PENANCES TO WIN YOU. HER CONCENTRATION IS UNSWERVING.

THEN VISHNU PLEADED.

O SHIVA, GRANT HER THE BOON SHE SEEKS AND MARRY HER.

SO BE IT!

THEIR MISSION ACCOMPLISHED, BRAHMA, VISHNU AND THE REST DEPARTED.

I SHALL GO TO SATI.

O DAUGHTER OF DAKSHA, I AM PLEASED BY YOUR DEVOTION! CHOOSE A BOON AND IT SHALL BE YOURS.

THOUGH SHIVA KNEW WHAT THE BOON WOULD BE, HE WANTED TO HEAR HER SPEAK.

HOW CAN I TELL HIM THAT HE IS THE BOON I SEEK?

SATI HESITATED BUT FOR A SECOND. THEN—

LORD, WILL YOU...

BUT SHIVA DID NOT LET HER COMPLETE HER QUESTION.

BE MY CONSORT, SATI.

FOR A WHILE SATI STOOD SMILING SWEETLY AT HIM. THEN—

LORD, PLEASE TAKE ME WITH THE CONSENT AND THE BLESSINGS OF MY FATHER.

SO BE IT!

WHEN SHIVA REACHED KAILAS, HE SENT FOR BRAHMA.

I HAVE GRANTED SATI THE BOON SHE SOUGHT. NOW YOU GO AND SPEAK TO DAKSHA.

BRAHMA SUCCEEDED IN PERSUADING DAKSHA.

LET HIM COME TO ME ON AN AUSPICIOUS DAY AND I SHALL OFFER HIM MY DAUGHTER.

AND SATI WAS MARRIED TO SHIVA.

AFTER THE WEDDING, SHIVA TOOK SATI TO KAILAS WHERE THEY SPENT MANY A HAPPY DAY.

THEN ONE DAY—

THE SAGES AT PRAYAG ARE PERFORMING A GRAND YAGNA. ALL THE CELESTIAL BEINGS HAVE BEEN INVITED. WOULD YOU LIKE TO GO?

I WOULD, MY LORD!

SO SHIVA AND SATI WENT.

WHEN THEY ENTERED THE GROUNDS, THE DEVAS AND SAGES BOWED TO THEM.

COME, SATI. LET US SIT AT THE PLACE ASSIGNED TO US.

AS SOON AS THEY WERE SEATED, DAKSHA ENTERED.

HA! THEY RECOGNISE ME AS THE CHIEF PRAJAPATI.

WHAT! MY VILE SON-IN-LAW REMAINS SEATED! HE DARES TO INSULT ME. I SHALL TEACH HIM A LESSON.

MY FATHER-IN-LAW DOES NOT REALISE THAT IF I, HIS SUPERIOR, BOW TO HIM, HARM WILL BEFALL HIM.

AFTER THE SACRIFICE WHEN DAKSHA REACHED HIS ABODE, HE COULD HARDLY WAIT TO AVENGE HIS HUMILIATION.

I WILL HOLD THE GREATEST YAGNA EVER WITNESSED. BRAHMA AND VISHNU SHALL BE ESCORTED TO IT. I WILL INVITE ALL THE INHABITANTS OF THE THREE WORLDS. BUT NOT MY UNCOUTH SON-IN-LAW AND THE UNGRATEFUL DAUGHTER WHO CHOSE HIM.

A FEW DAYS LATER—

WHERE ARE THEY GOING IN SUCH HASTE—AND DECKED IN THEIR FINEST ATTIRE?

I'LL FIND OUT.

WHEN SHE LEARNT THAT THEY WERE ON THEIR WAY TO DAKSHA'S GRAND YAGNA—

HOW STRANGE THAT MY MISTRESS AND THE LORD HAVE NOT BEEN INVITED!

SHE RETURNED TO SATI.

THEY ARE ON THEIR WAY TO A GRAND YAGNA, YOUR FATHER IS PERFORMING.

MY FATHER?

SATI WAS SURPRISED.

HOW COULD FATHER FORGET TO INVITE US?

SHE WENT TO SHIVA AND TOLD HIM ABOUT THE SACRIFICE.

LET US GO TO MY FATHER'S SACRIFICIAL HALL.

SHIVA LOOKED LOVINGLY AT HER.

WE CANNOT, DEAR ONE. DAKSHA CONSIDERS ME HIS ENEMY. WE HAVE DELIBER-ATELY BEEN OVERLOOKED.

BUT SATI PERSISTED.

ALL THE SAME I WOULD LIKE TO GO.

SHIVA KNEW THAT NO GOOD WOULD COME OF HER VISIT. BUT SHE WAS HIS EQUAL.

I WILL NOT COME. BUT IF YOU REALLY MUST GO, I WILL WILLINGLY SEND YOU —AND IN ROYAL SPLEN-DOUR. NANDI, MY AT-TENDANT, WILL CARRY YOU THERE.

SO SATI SET OUT ON NANDI, SHIVA'S FAVOURITE ATTENDANT.

AT THE GATES OF DAKSHA'S ABODE, SATI DISMOUNTED AND WALKED UP TO HER FATHER. BUT HE IGNORED HER PRESENCE.

YET SATI, EVER DUTIFUL, BOWED TO HER PARENTS.

THEN—

WHY WERE MY LORD AND I NOT INVITED?

WHEN DAKSHA DID NOT REPLY, SHE TURNED UPON VISHNU AND BRAHMA.

HOW COULD YOU TOLERATE THIS INSULT TO MY LORD? YOU WHO···

BUT DAKSHA CRUELLY CUT HER SHORT.

SATI! I'VE HAD ENOUGH OF YOUR IMPUDENCE. YOU MAY GO OR STAY. WHY DID YOU COME AT ALL?

HIS ANGER MOUNTED AS HE SPOKE OF SHIVA.

YOUR HUSBAND IS UNCOUTH. HE IS NOT FIT TO BE PRESENT ON SUCH AN AUSPICIOUS OCCASION. I GAVE YOU TO HIM ONLY BECAUSE MY FATHER PERSUADED ME TO.

THEN HE BECAME CALMER.

ANYWAY, NOW THAT YOU HAVE COME, FORGET HIM. SIT DOWN AND ACCEPT A SHARE OF THE SACRIFICIAL OFFERINGS.

SATI, FOR A MOMENT, STOOD SPEECHLESS WITH SHAME AND ANGER.

WHY? OH WHY DID I INSIST ON COMING?

THEN SHE TURNED UPON HER FATHER.

YOU ARE VAIN AND WICKED. I AM ASHAMED TO CALL MYSELF YOUR DAUGHTER.

I WILL CAST OFF THIS BODY OF MINE AS A WORTHLESS CORPSE.

THEN, BECOMING CALMER, SHE FIXED HER MIND ON HER LORD.

MY LORD, I SHALL COME BACK TO YOU WHEN I AM RE-BORN OF A FATHER I CAN RESPECT.

AND INVOKING YOGIC FLAMES, SATI IMMOLATED HER BODY IN THEM.

ALAS! SHIVA'S BELOVED HAS GIVEN UP HER BODY.

ALAS!

ALAS!

CRUEL DAKSHA WILL HAVE TO PAY FOR THIS.

HER ATTENDANTS, WHO WERE WAITING OUTSIDE, HEARD THESE CRIES AND CHARGED IN.

FIE ON THE EVIL PRAJAPATI!

WHERE IS HE?

THEY RUSHED TOWARDS DAKSHA.

DON'T SPARE A HAIR ON HIS HEAD.

BUT THE SAGE, BHRIGU, IMMEDIATELY POURED OFFERINGS INTO THE SACRIFICIAL FIRE...

... AND INVOKED THOUSANDS OF POWERFUL DEMONS.

A TERRIBLE FIGHT ENSUED.

SHIVA'S ATTENDANTS WERE DEFEATED...

...AND HAD TO RETREAT.

WHEN THEY REACHED KAILAS —

O LORD, THE WICKED DAKSHA HUMILIATED SATI AND SPOKE ILL OF YOU.

SATI BECAME ANGRY. AFTER CENSURING HER FATHER SHE BURNT UP HER BODY.

WE BECAME INFURIATED AND ATTACKED BUT WERE ROUTED BY BHRIGU'S DEMONS.

SHIVA WAS FURIOUS.

HE PLUCKED OUT A CLUSTER OF HIS MATTED HAIR AND···

...DASHED IT TO THE GROUND.

BOOM

THE CLUSTER SPLIT IN TWO.

FROM ONE HALF AROSE THE POWERFUL VIRABHADRA AND...

...FROM THE OTHER THE TERRIBLE MAHAKALI.

LORD, COMMAND ME QUICKLY! WHAT AM I TO DO?

MAY VICTORY BE YOURS.

DESTROY THE SACRIFICE OF THE CONCEITED DAKSHA. KILL HIM AND RETURN. TAKE AS MANY OF MY ATTENDANTS AS YOU NEED.

EAGER TO CARRY OUT THE COMMAND, VIRABHADRA SET OFF AT ONCE FOR DAKSHA'S ABODE WITH MAHAKALI LEADING THE HORDES.

SUDDENLY—

LOOK! SHIVA'S HORDES!

VIRABHADRA!

MAHAKALI!

DAKSHA APPEALED TO INDRA, KING OF THE DEVAS.

I NOW DEPEND ON YOUR STRENGTH AND SUPPORT ALONE. SAVE MY SACRIFICE AND MY LIFE.

INDRA IMMEDIATELY MOUNTED HIS ELEPHANT AND LED THE DEVAS.

A TERRIBLE BATTLE IT WAS.

BHRIGU ONCE AGAIN INVOKED HIS DEMONS. BUT THEY WERE QUELLED.

COME! COME NEAR ME! LET ME CUT YOU TO PIECES.

COME, AGNI! COME, YAMA! COME, O VALIANT ONES.

MANY OF THE DEVAS AND CELESTIAL SAGES DESERTED AND FLED TO HEAVEN.

OUR RACE WILL BE WIPED OUT. LET US FLEE.

BUT INDRA DID NOT GIVE UP. HE ATTACKED NANDI.

NANDI PIERCED HIM WITH HIS TRIDENT.

INDRA RETALIATED WITH HIS THUNDERBOLT, AND NANDI FELL.

VIRABHADRA WAS FURIOUS TO SEE SHIVA'S FAVOURITE LYING UNCONSCIOUS.

HE DREW HIS BOW AND LET FLY HIS DEADLY ARROWS.

SEVERELY WOUNDED, EVEN INDRA HAD TO FLEE.

LOOK! OUR LEADER IS RETREATING. WE ARE LOST.

THEN VISHNU CAME FORWARD, TOOK INDRA'S POSITION AND FACED VIRABHADRA.

BUT VIRABHADRA CHARGED WITH HIS TRIDENT AND VISHNU FELL UNCONSCIOUS.

LEAVING HIM THERE, VIRABHADRA WENT IN SEARCH OF DAKSHA.

HA! THERE YOU ARE, EVIL ONE!

HE TORE OFF DAKSHA'S HEAD AND...

...THREW IT INTO THE SACRIFICIAL FIRE.

HIS TASK ACCOMPLISHED, HE RETURNED TO KAILAS.

AS VIRABHADRA LEFT, COOL FRAGRANT BREEZES BLEW, REVIVING ALL THOSE WHO HAD FALLEN.

BRAHMA CAME UP TO VISHNU.

MY SON MUST BE BROUGHT TO LIFE AND THE YAGNA COMPLETED. WHAT SHOULD WE DO?

LET'S GO TO SHIVA'S ABODE AND PROPITIATE HIM.

WHEN THEY REACHED SHIVA'S ABODE ON MOUNT KAILAS —

GREAT ONE! YOU ARE MERCIFUL. LET THE INCOMPLETE YAGNA OF DAKSHA BE COMPLETED. LET HIM BE RESTORED TO LIFE.

DAKSHA ALLOWED HATE TO BECOME HIS MASTER. IF ONE HATES ANOTHER IT WILL RECOIL ON ONESELF. DAKSHA SHALL BE REVIVED, BUT WITH THE HEAD OF A GOAT.

THEN COME TO THE SACRIFICIAL ALTAR WITH US, O LORD.

I SHALL.

WHEN THEY REACHED THE VENUE OF THE SACRIFICE—

BRING ME THE HEAD OF THE SACRIFICIAL GOAT.

THE HEAD WAS BROUGHT. SHIVA JOINED IT TO DAKSHA'S NECK.

DAKSHA SLOWLY AROSE AS IF FROM A DEEP SLEEP.

WHEN HE SAW SHIVA, HE BOWED BEFORE HIM.

I HAVE BEEN WICKED AND FOOLISH. YOU HAVE PUNISHED ME. I PRAY NOW THAT I BE PERMITTED TO COMPLETE MY YAGNA.

WITH SHIVA'S PERMISSION AND GRACIOUS BLESSINGS, DAKSHA COMPLETED THE YAGNA.

AT KAILAS, SHIVA WENT INTO MEDIATATION TILL···

···SATI, TRUE TO HER WORD, WAS REBORN AS PARVATI TO HIMAVAN, A FATHER SHE COULD LOVE AND RESPECT AND WHO LOVED AND RESPECTED HER. AND AS PARVATI SHE WOOED AND WON SHIVA, NEVER TO BE SEPARATED FROM HIM AGAIN.

SHIVA PARVATI

SHIVA'S FATHER-IN-LAW, DAKSHA, FOR SOME REASON DISLIKED HIM AND NEVER LOST AN OPPORTUNITY TO INSULT HIM. SATI, SHIVA'S WIFE, ASHAMED OF BEING THE DAUGHTER OF SUCH A FATHER, GAVE UP HER BODY. AFTER SATI'S DEATH, SHIVA WENT BACK TO HIS MEDITATION ON THE HIMALAYAS.

VERY NEAR THE GROVE WHERE SHIVA MEDITATED, LIVED THE GREAT MOUNTAIN KING, HIMAVAT.

HE HAD MARRIED THE HEAVENLY NYMPH MENAKA.

THEY WERE LOVED DEARLY BY ALL.

ONE DAY —

MENAKA HAS HAD A BABY GIRL! A LOVELY CHILD!

LET US CALL HER PARVATI.

NATURE TOO REJOICED AT PARVATI'S BIRTH.

WHAT A BEAUTIFUL CHILD SHE IS!

HUSH! DO NOT PROVOKE THE EVIL SPIRITS.

PARVATI WAS REALLY SATI WHO HAD BEEN REBORN, BUT THIS TIME TO A FATHER SHE COULD BE PROUD OF AND WHO WAS PROUD OF HER.

SHE WAS AS LIVELY AS SHE WAS LOVELY AND HAD MANY FRIENDS.

PARVATI! CATCH HA! HA! YOU MISSED AGAIN.

I HAVE HAD ENOUGH OF THIS GAME. COME LET US GO HOME AND PLAY WITH OUR DOLLS.

THE YEARS FLEW BY AND PARVATI GREW UP TO BE A BEAUTIFUL MAIDEN.

PARVATI, MY CHILD, IT IS TIME YOU WERE MARRIED!

MOTHER!

THAT NIGHT —

IT IS HIGH TIME WE FOUND A HUSBAND FOR PARVATI.

I KNOW. BUT I CANNOT THINK OF ANY ONE WORTHY ENOUGH.

HIMAVAT DOTED ON HIS DAUGHTER. ONLY THE BEST WAS GOOD ENOUGH FOR HER.

I WILL GIVE MY PEERLESS CHILD TO ONE WORTHY OF HER IN EVERY RESPECT.

ONE DAY THE SAGE NARADA VISITED HIMAVAT.

NARAYANA! NARAYANA!

PARVATI! COME HERE.

COMING, FATHER.

WHEN PARVATI RETURNED TO HER FRIENDS —

YOUR DAUGHTER IS DESTINED TO BE THE WIFE OF NONE OTHER THAN THE MIGHTY LORD SHIVA.

HOW CAN I APPROACH SHIVA? SUPPOSING HE REFUSES ME? HE HAS NOT LOOKED UPON A WOMAN SINCE SATI GAVE UP HER BODY...

...AND YET I DO NOT WISH TO SEEK FURTHER. NARADA'S PROPHECIES ALWAYS COME TRUE. I'LL WAIT AND SEE.

SO HIMAVAT WAITED. BUT ONE FINE DAY —

I HAVE WAITED LONG ENOUGH, AND SHIVA CONTINUES TO BE LOST IN MEDITATION.

SUDDENLY AN IDEA STRUCK HIM. HE WENT TO MENAKA.

I WILL SEND PARVATI TO WAIT UPON SHIVA. HE WILL NOT BE ABLE TO RESIST HER CHARMS.

AN EXCELLENT IDEA!

HIMAVAT CALLED PARVATI TO HIM.

MY BELOVED CHILD, WILL YOU, WITH YOUR FRIENDS, WAIT UPON LORD SHIVA, WHO MEDITATES IN YONDER GROVE?

WE HAVE OFTEN SEEN HIM, FATHER. WE SHALL GO.

HIMAVAT TOOK PARVATI AND TWO OF HER FRIENDS AND WENT UP TO SHIVA.

LORD, YOU HAVE NONE TO HELP YOU FOR YOUR RITUALS. MY DAUGHTER CAN.

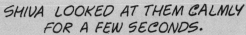

SHIVA LOOKED AT THEM CALMLY FOR A FEW SECONDS.

LET THE GIRLS SERVE ME. THEY ARE NO HINDRANCE TO ONE WHO HAS RENOUNCED THE WORLD.

THEN HE ADDRESSED HIMAVAT.

I AM GRATEFUL TO YOU FOR YOUR THOUGHTFUL GESTURE. LET THE MAIDS SERVE ME AS THEY WILL.

HIMAVAT WAS JUBILANT AS HE LEFT THE MAIDS AND WENT.

NARADA'S PROPHECY WILL COME TRUE VERY SHORTLY. I AM ASSURED OF PARVATI'S FUTURE.

PARVATI BEGAN TO ATTEND ON SHIVA.

PARVATI, HAVE YOU COLLECTED THE FLOWERS FOR TODAY'S WORSHIP?

HERE THEY ARE, MY LORD.

PARVATI, COME ON. LET US FEED THE DEER.

A MOMENT. LET ME FINISH CLEANING THE LORD'S PRAYER SEAT.

SHE CAREFULLY CHOSE THE 'KUSA' GRASS FOR HIS RITES ...

COME FARTHER! THE BEST GRASS GROWS THERE.

OH! PARVATI, WE ARE TIRED.

... AND FANNED HIM GENTLY WHEN THE DAY GREW WARM.

PARVATI! HAVEN'T YOU FINISHED? COME!

MY FRIENDS CALL ME. BUT I WOULD RATHER SERVE THE LORD.

WHEN I AM TIRED I ONLY HAVE TO GAZE AT THE PALE MOON ON HIS FOREHEAD AND I AM REVIVED. WHAT POWER IS THIS?

THUS PARVATI GREW TO LOVE SHIVA WITH ALL HER HEART.

MEANWHILE THERE WAS TROUBLE IN HEAVEN. THE GODS LED BY INDRA CAME TO BRAHMA.

WELCOME, MY SONS. BUT WHY DO YOU LOOK SO SAD AND GLOOMY?

9

INDRA SIGNALLED TO BRIHASPATI, THEIR CHIEF PRIEST, TO SPEAK.

TARAKA, THE WICKED ASURA, HAS BECOME A MENACE.

HE HAS SEIZED HEAVEN, OUR ABODE AND IS TERRORIZING OUR PEOPLE.

INDRA STEPPED FORWARD —

I EVEN SEND HIM GIFTS TO FLATTER HIM AND WIN HIS GOODWILL.

THEN BRIHASPATI CONTINUED —

BUT THE MORE WE TRY TO PLEASE HIM THE MORE RUTHLESS HE BECOMES.

10

"HE HAS LAID WASTE ALL OUR BEAUTIFUL GARDENS AND OUR CAPTIVE WOMENFOLK TEARFULLY FAN HIM WHILE HE SLEEPS?"

WE HAVE COME TO ASK YOU TO GIVE US A CHIEF WHO WILL LEAD US AGAINST HIM.

BRAHMA WAS HELPLESS.

DEAR SONS, MUCH AS I WANT TO HELP YOU, I CAN'T.

TARAKA HAS BECOME POWERFUL BY VIRTUE OF THE BOON I ONCE GRANTED HIM. SO I CANNOT DESTROY HIM.

BUT HE HAD A SOLUTION.

SHIVA IS DESTINED TO MARRY PARVATI.

GO! MAKE HIM AWARE OF HER BEAUTY.

THEN BRAHMA PROMISED —

THE SON BORN AFTER THEIR WEDDING WILL BE YOUR **WAR-LORD** AND KILL TARAKA.

INDRA WENT STRAIGHT TO KAMA, THE GOD OF LOVE.

WHAT CAN I DO FOR YOU, MY LORD?

I WANT YOU TO LURE SHIVA INTO MARRYING PARVATI.

IT SHALL BE DONE.

COME RATI, MY BELOVED WIFE AND SPRING, MY BOSOM COMPANION. LET US GO TO SHIVA'S GROVE.

BUT AS THEY APPROACHED SHIVA'S GROVE AND KAMA SAW THE MIGHTY SHIVA—

MY COURAGE FAILS ME!

AT THAT MOMENT PARVATI PASSED BY AND KAMA REGAINED COURAGE.

WITH SUCH AN ALLY I CANNOT FAIL.

PARVATI BOWED AND PLACED SOME FLOWERS BEFORE SHIVA, WHO HAD JUST COME OUT OF A DIVINE TRANCE.

MAY YOU BE BLESSED, SWEET MAID, WITH A HUSBAND WHO LOVES NONE BUT YOU.

SHIVA HAS SPOKEN AND HE CANNOT LIE. I AM SO HAPPY.

PARVATI WAS ABOUT TO PLACE A LOTUS GARLAND AROUND SHIVA'S NECK WHEN ···

AH! THE TIME IS RIPE.

KAMA'S ARROW FOUND IT'S MARK.

WHAT A BEAUTIFUL CREATURE IS SHE WHO SERVES ME! WHY HAVE I NOT BEEN AWARE OF THIS?

WHY DO I BLUSH WHEN THE LORD LOOKS AT ME? I FEEL STRANGE.

BUT WITH A GREAT EFFORT SHIVA BROUGHT HIS EMOTIONS UNDER CONTROL, AND LOOKED AROUND.

WHO HAS DARED DISTURB THE PEACE IN MY SOUL?

HE SAW KAMA AND ANGER FILLED HIS BEING.

HE LOOKED AT KAMA AND THAT GOD WAS BURNT TO ASHES.

ONE LOOK AT HIM AND RATI FAINTED.

WITHOUT SO MUCH AS LOOKING AT PARVATI, SHIVA LEFT THE GROVE.

PARVATI WAS OVERCOME WITH GRIEF AND SHAME.

NOT ONLY HAVE I LOVED IN VAIN BUT MY BELOVED HAS SPURNED ME BEFORE MY PLAYMATES!

HIMAVAT CAME AND PARVATI RAN TO HIM. HE HELD HER TENDERLY.

DEAR CHILD!

FATHER.

THEY MADE THEIR WAY HOMEWARD, SLOWLY AND SADLY.

IN THE MEANWHILE RATI WOKE UP FROM HER FAINT.

OF WHAT USE IS LIFE TO ME WHEN MY KAMA IS DEAD? IT WERE BETTER I TOO DIED AND JOINED HIM.

BUT A HEAVENLY VOICE STOPPED HER.

LIVE OH WIDOWED LADY. PARVATI WILL YET WIN SHIVA BY PENANCE, AND YOUR HUSBAND WILL BE RESTORED TO YOU ON THEIR WEDDING DAY.

RATI, CONSOLED AND CHEERED BY THE VOICE, LIVED AND WAITED FOR KAMA.

PARVATI WAS EXTREMELY PAINED BY SHIVA'S BEHAVIOUR BUT SHE CONTINUED TO LOVE HIM.

MY BEAUTY HAS FAILED TO MOVE HIM.

BUT I WILL NOT GIVE UP. SHIVA MAY NOT VALUE BEAUTY BUT PENANCE AND DEVOTION WILL CERTAINLY WIN HIM.

SHE TOLD HER MOTHER OF HER DECISION.

BUT WHY, MY CHILD? ARE THERE NO GODS TO LOVE YOU HERE? GIVE HIM UP.

MOTHER, YOU CANNOT UNDERSTAND. I HAVE DECIDED. PLEASE BLESS ME.

AND MENAKA SHAKING HER HEAD BLESSED PARVATI.

PARVATI THEN WENT TO HIMAVAT.

FATHER, GIVE ME YOUR CONSENT AND A GROVE THAT I MIGHT SPEND MY DAYS IN PENANCE AND PRAYER.

SO BE IT, MY BELOVED CHILD.

CASTING OFF HER FINE CLOTHES AND JEWELLERY, PARVATI ENTERED THE GROVE HER FATHER GAVE HER.

THE DEER IN THE GROVE LOVED HER.

SHE SLEPT ON THE COLD DAMP GROUND AND BARELY ATE ANYTHING.

DO YOU FAIL TO UNDERSTAND MY LOVE? I DON'T BELIEVE IT. PERHAPS YOU WISH TO TRY ME FURTHER.

AS SHE PERFORMED HER RITES, THE HERMITS NEARBY OFTEN CAME TO WATCH...

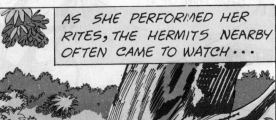

...AND MARVELLED.

18

GRADUALLY SHE GAVE UP EVEN THE LITTLE SHE ATE.

SHE HAS EATEN NOTHING SINCE WEEKS.

SHE IS *APARNA

* LADY OF THE UNBROKEN FAST.

I WILL SUBSIST ON YOUR NAME RESTING ON MY LIPS.

SHE SAT IN AN ICY POOL, HER LIPS QUIVERING, AND CONCENTRATED ON HER LORD.

TRULY SHE IS THE ASCETIC OF ASCETICS.

YOUR IMAGE FIXED IN MY HEART SHALL WARM ME.

MANY YEARS PASSED BUT PARVATI NEVER ONCE GAVE UP HOPE.

ONE DAY WHILE SHE WAS PERFORMING HER RITUALS BEFORE ENTERING THE POOL, A YOUNG HERMIT CAME TO SEE HER. PARVATI BOWED TO HIM.

HOW CAN YOUR TENDER FRAME CARRY OUT THE TASK YOUR SPIRIT HAS SET IT?

19

ALL HER AUSTERITY HAD ONLY ENHANCED PARVATI'S EXQUISITE BEAUTY.

TRULY YOU HAVE PROVED TO THE WORLD THAT BEAUTY AND PURITY NEED NOT DESTROY ONE ANOTHER.

YOUR DEEDS HAVE CROWNED YOUR FATHER WITH AN EVEN GREATER GLORY THAN HE ALREADY OWNED.

NOBLE MAIDEN, WHY HAVE YOU UNDERTAKEN SUCH SEVERE PENANCE?

IT IS COMMON FOR A LONELY PERSON TORN BY GRIEF AND ANGUISH TO LIVE A HERMIT'S LIFE.

BUT WHY SHOULD YOU OH FAULTLESS ONE, LOVED AND CHERISHED BY ALL, DO SO?

HEARING THIS PARVATI HEAVED A HEAVY SIGH.

AH! IS IT BECAUSE OF UNREQUITED LOVE? NO, THAT'S NOT POSSIBLE. A PRICELESS GEM LIKE YOU IS SOUGHT AND DOES NOT SEEK.

GO HOME FAIR MAIDEN. I WILL GIVE YOU HALF THE MERITS I'VE EARNED IF YOU STOP THIS PENANCE. BUT PRAY TELL ME THE REASON.

PARVATI TURNED TO HER FRIEND FOR HELP.

THE MAID TOLD ALL.

SHE HAD SET HER HEART ON WINNING SHIVA'S LOVE. SHE FAILED TO WIN HIM BY HER BEAUTY. SO SHE DECIDED TO DO IT BY PENANCE AND AUSTERITY.

SHE OFTEN CRIES OUT TO HIM BUT SHIVA HAS REMAINED DEAF TO HER APPEALS.

THE HERMIT TURNED TO PARVATI.

IS THIS TRUE? OR IS YOUR FRIEND JOKING?

OH HOLY ONE, IT IS TRUE! I ADORE GREAT SHIVA. I AM SURE, I WILL WIN HIS LOVE BY MY PENANCE AND DEVOTION.

OH-H! LADY, I KNOW SHIVA. HE IS COVERED WITH ASHES AND SERPENTS DECK HIS BODY, WHICH IS CLOTHED IN FOUL-SMELLING HIDES.

HOW CAN YOUR SWEET AND TENDER SELF BECOME HIS BRIDE? HE IS DEFORMED, UNCOUTH AND POOR. HIS ANCESTRY IS UNKNOWN.

HE IS NOT FIT FOR YOU. GIVE HIM UP AND CHOOSE SOME ONE ELSE MORE WORTHY OF ...

STOP!

PARVATI COULD NO LONGER CONTROL HER ANGER.

IT TAKES A GREAT SOUL TO KNOW A GREAT SOUL.

LOW CREATURES CAN NEVER UNDERSTAND LOFTY MOTIVES. YOUR TONGUE GIVES AWAY YOUR EVIL MIND.

SHIVA NEITHER IMPRESSES NOR IS IMPRESSED BY OUTWARD APPEARANCES. HIS VALUES ARE DIFFERENT FROM YOURS.

WHAT IF HE IS UNCOUTH POOR AND ILL-CLAD? WHAT IF SERPENTS DECK HIS BODY? HE IS MY CHOSEN LORD.

HIS FAILINGS MAY BE MANY AND HIS VIRTUES FEW, BUT I LOVE HIM.

THEN PARVATI TURNED TO HER FRIEND WHO LISTENED IN AWE.

DEAR MAID, ASK HIM TO GO AWAY. WHY SHOULD HE DEFILE HIS HEART WITH SUCH SLANDER?

BESIDES, THOUGH IT IS A SIN TO UTTER EVIL WORDS IT IS A GREATER SIN TO WAIT AND LISTEN. COME LET US GO.

AS PARVATI TURNED ANGRILY AWAY...

..THE HERMIT RUSHED FORWARD AND BLOCKED HER PATH.

?

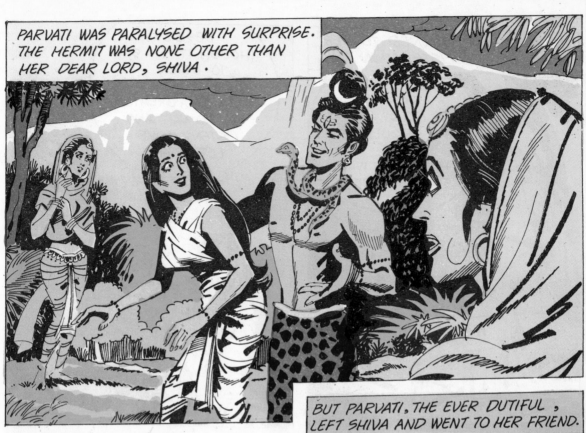

PARVATI WAS PARALYSED WITH SURPRISE. THE HERMIT WAS NONE OTHER THAN HER DEAR LORD, SHIVA.

OH! GENTLE MAIDEN, YOUR PENANCE AND DEVOTION HAVE WON ME. I BOW TO YOU, YOUR WILLING SLAVE.

BUT PARVATI, THE EVER DUTIFUL, LEFT SHIVA AND WENT TO HER FRIEND.

TELL HIM THAT MY FATHER SHOULD BE APPROACHED FOR MY HAND.

26

THE MAID DID SO AND PARVATI CAME BACK TO SHIVA.

DEAR ONE, I SHALL LOSE NO TIME.

THUS ASSURED, PARVATI WITH HER FRIEND TURNED HOMEWARD.

SHIVA CALLED FOR THE SEVEN RISHIS.

BRAHMA HAS PROMISED THE GODS THAT MY SON SHALL LEAD THEM AGAINST TARAKA.

TO FULFIL HIS PROMISE I WISH TO MARRY PARVATI. GO AND ASK HIMAVAT FOR HER HAND.

HIMAVAT OF COURSE WAS DELIGHTED.

AND THE WEDDING TOOK PLACE.

WHEN THE CEREMONY WAS OVER, THE GODS CAME TO SHIVA.

WE BEG YOU TO RESTORE KAMA TO RATI. FOR THE SAKE OF YOUR LOVELY BRIDE, HAVE PITY ON THE TENDER GOD AND HIS MOURNING WIFE.

I WILL. AM I NOT KAMA'S SLAVE TOO, NOW?

MANY YEARS PASSED AND SHIVA WAS LOST IN HIS LOVE FOR HIS WIFE.

SO INDRA SENT AGNI TO SHIVA.

I HAVE COME TO REMIND YOU OF OUR NEED.

SHIVA GAVE AGNI A SEED IN HIS PALM.

WHEN THIS IS RIPE A CHILD WILL EMERGE HE SHALL BE YOUR WAR-LORD.

AGNI TOOK THE SEED BUT IT WAS SO HOT, HE COULD BARELY HOLD IT.

I MUST HASTEN TO INDRA.

29

BY THE TIME HE REACHED INDRA, HE BECAME PALE WITH DISCOMFORT.

I HAVE IT BUT I CAN NO LONGER BEAR IT.

INDRA FELT SORRY FOR HIM.

TAKE IT TO GANGA. SHE WILL COOL YOU AS WELL AS SUSTAIN IT.

AGNI WENT TO GANGA. BUT WHEN HE DIPPED HIMSELF AND THE SEED IN HER COOL WATERS, SHE BUBBLED AND BOILED OVER, AND THE SEED WAS THROWN ASHORE.

JUST THEN SIX CELESTIAL NYMPHS CAME TO BATHE IN THE GANGA.

WHAT IS THIS? A SEED?

LET US LAY IT IN A NEST OF SHARA GRASS.

THEY PICKED THE SEED AND PLACED IT NEAR SOME 'SHARA' GRASS.

THE SEED AT THAT MOMENT WAS RIPE AND KARTIKEYA EMERGED. THE CHILD GREW SIX FACES TO CHUCKLE AT EACH OF THE SIX NYMPHS WHO GAZED AT IT IN WONDER.

WE SHALL TAKE HIM WITH US. WE SAW HIM FIRST.

JUST THEN GANGA CAME OUT IN THE FORM OF A WOMAN AND AGNI TOO APPEARED.

I'WILL TAKE HIM. I BORE HIM.

NO! HE IS PROMISED TO US.

AT THAT MOMENT SHIVA AND PARVATI REACHED THE SCENE. SHIVA SETTLED THE MATTER.

WHO ELSE BUT PARVATI IS THE FIT ONE TO BRING UP A CHILD DESTINED TO LEAD THE GODS?

PARVATI PICKED THE CHILD UP TENDERLY AND CLASPED IT TO HER.

AND LED BY SHIVA RETURNED TO MOUNT KAILAS.

IN TIME KARTIKEYA GREW UP AND LED THE GODS IN A FIERCE BATTLE AGAINST THE EVIL TARAKA AND SLEW HIM.

INDRA WAS RESTORED TO THE THRONE, AND HAPPINESS REIGNED ONCE MORE IN HEAVEN.

SHIVA AND ARJUNA

QUIET, PEACEFUL INDRAKEELA, IN THE HIMALAYAS WAS A RETREAT OF ASCETICS.

ONE DAY —

WHO COULD THIS STRANGER BE?

DOESN'T HE KNOW THAT WEAPONS HAVE NO PLACE HERE?

THE YOUNG ASCETICS FOLLOWED THE STRANGER TO THE RIVER BANK AND WATCHED HIM CLOSELY.

LOOK AT HIS BOW! COULD HE BE ARJUNA, THE PANDAVA?

IF HE IS, WHY IS HE HERE?

THE PANDAVAS ARE IN EXILE, HAVING LOST THE GAME OF DICE TO THE WILY DURYODHANA.

PERHAPS THE POOR PANDAVA IS SEEKING DIVINE GRACE!

IT WAS INDEED ARJUNA WHO WAS THERE TO PROPITIATE LORD SHIVA.

OM NAMO SHIVAYA *

FOR DAYS HE PERSISTED.

OM NAMO SHIVAYA.

* SALUTATIONS TO SHIVA

FOUR MONTHS LATER —

WE CANNOT GO ANY NEARER.

THE HEAT OF THE TERRIBLE PENANCE IS SPREADING FAR AND WIDE.

IT SOON CHOKED THE WHOLE FOREST.

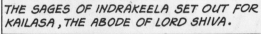

THE SAGES OF INDRAKEELA SET OUT FOR KAILASA, THE ABODE OF LORD SHIVA.

AT KAILASA —

LORD, GRANT ARJUNA HIS WISH, AND RELIEVE US OF THIS SUFFERING.

SO BE IT.

WHEN THE SAGES DEPARTED —

WHAT DOES ARJUNA WANT, MY LORD?

HE WANTS CELESTIAL WEAPONS.

CAN HE WIELD THEM, MY LORD?

I WILL FIND OUT BY TESTING HIM.

I'LL APPEAR BEFORE HIM AS A KIRATA* AND ENGAGE HIM IN A DUEL.

MAY I ACCOMPANY YOU?

YOU MAY, BUT IN DISGUISE.

I SHALL COME AS A KIRATA-WOMAN.

* HUNTER

WHEN THE HORDES OF SHIVA HEARD ABOUT IT—

LORD, WE WOULD LIKE TO WITNESS THE GREAT COMBAT. MAY WE ACCOMPANY YOU?

YOU MAY, IN THE GUISE OF KIRATA WOMEN.

SOON—

AS THEY APPROACHED INDRAKEELA—

SEE THAT BOAR RUNNING WILD, MY LORD.

HAH! A FIT TARGET FOR MY ARROW!

BUT THE WILY, SWIFT BOAR OUTDISTANCED THE KIRATA...

...AND CHARGED INTO THE QUIET HERMITAGE, DRIVING THE ASCETICS HELTER-SKELTER.

IT IS MOOKASURA AGAIN! NOW IN THE FORM OF A BOAR!

HIS PENANCE DISTURBED BY THE DIN, ARJUNA OPENED HIS EYES...

...RAISED HIS BOW AND TOOK AIM.

STOP! IT'S MINE. LEAVE IT TO ME. I WAS STALKING IT.

* DEMON MOOKA

THE WILD EXULTATION OF THE KIRATA WOMEN AMUSED ARJUNA.

O KIRATA, DOES NOT THIS THICK FOREST TERRIFY YOUR WOMEN FOLK? AND YOU THEIR ONLY ESCORT?

YOUNG MAN, WE FEAR NOTHING.

PERHAPS YOU ARE TERRIFIED. YOU DO APPEAR SOFT!

SOFT? ME? DIDN'T YOU SEE THE FORCE OF MY ARROW PIERCING THE BOAR?

IT WAS OUR CHIEF'S ARROW THAT KILLED THE BOAR.

THEY SPEAK THE TRUTH, YOUNG MAN. YOUR ARROW HIT A DEAD BOAR.

ARJUNA WAS ENRAGED.

ALL RIGHT, KIRATA. WE WILL SETTLE ONCE AND FOR ALL WHO IS THE BETTER SHOT.

ARROWS WHIZZED PAST AS THE TWO ARCHERS MATCHED THEIR SKILLS.

AFTER A WHILE —

MY QUIVER IS EMPTY AND NOT A SCRATCH YET ON THE KIRATA.

O MIGHTY ARCHER, SHALL I LEND YOU A FEW ARROWS?

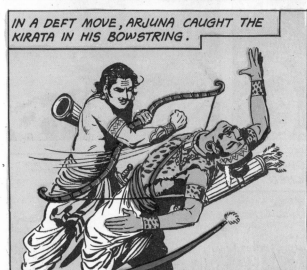

IN A DEFT MOVE, ARJUNA CAUGHT THE KIRATA IN HIS BOWSTRING.

THE NEXT MOMENT, THE KIRATA WRESTED THE BOW FROM ARJUNA...

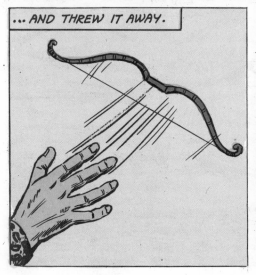

... AND THREW IT AWAY.

THE KIRATA WOMEN DANCED FOR JOY.

THE ASCETIC IS BEATEN!

10

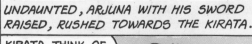

UNDAUNTED, ARJUNA WITH HIS SWORD RAISED, RUSHED TOWARDS THE KIRATA.

KIRATA, THINK OF THE LORD AT THE LAST MOMENT OF YOUR LIFE AND PREPARE TO DIE.

AS ARJUNA SMOTE THE HEAD OF THE KIRATA WITH HIS HEAVY SWORD, IT BROKE.

SHORN OF HIS ARMS, ARJUNA CONTINUED THE FIGHT WITH UPROOTED TREES.

BUT THE KIRATA REMAINED UNSCATHED.

IN A DESPERATE ATTEMPT, ARJUNA CHARGED AT THE KIRATA WITH BARE HANDS.

WITH A FLICK OF HIS WRIST, THE KIRATA LIFTED ARJUNA...

...AND FLUNG HIM DOWN.

A HUMBLED ARJUNA THOUGHT OF SHIVA AND HIS GRACE.

RIGHT ON THE SPOT HE MADE A LINGA...

...AND BEGAN TO WORSHIP IT.

A NEW POWER SURGED THROUGH HIS LIMBS.

A REJUVENATED ARJUNA AGAIN CHALLENGED HIS RIVAL.

KIRATA, YOUR TIME IS UP!

BUT HE STOPPED, AS IF TRANSFIXED.

THE FLOWERS, I OFFERED TO MY LORD SHIVA, ON YOUR HEAD! I SEE NOW. YOU ARE NONE OTHER THAN HIM!

ARJUNA FELL AT THE FEET OF THE KIRATA.

O LORD, PARDON ME AND MY VANITY.

SHIVA THEN REVEALED HIMSELF IN HIS TRUE FORM AND SO DID PARVATI IN HERS.

I AM PLEASED WITH YOUR DEVOTION AND COURAGE. I SHALL IMPART TO YOU THE SECRET OF THE PASHU-PATA MISSILE WHICH WILL HELP YOU IN THE HOUR OF NEED.

SHIVA'S WORD CAME TRUE. LATER IN THE MAHABHARATA WAR, IT WAS ONLY WITH THE PASHUPATA THAT ARJUNA COULD KILL HIS ARCH-RIVAL, KARNA.

SHIVA THE FISHERMAN

ONCE IN KAILASA, SHIVA STARTED EXPOUNDING THE MYSTERY OF THE VEDAS TO PARVATI WHO WAS LISTENING ATTENTIVELY.

YEARS PASSED BY. SHIVA CONTINUED WITHOUT A BREAK.

GRADUALLY, IN SPITE OF HER BEST EFFORTS, PARVATI'S ATTENTION FLAGGED AND SHIVA WAS ANNOYED.

THE VEDAS ARE NOT FOR YOU. SINCE YOU ARE NO BETTER THAN A COMMON FISHERWOMAN...

...MAY YOU BE BORN AS ONE!

BUT WHEN PARVATI VANISHED, THE VERY NEXT MOMENT —

WHAT HAVE I DONE!

IN THOUGHTLESS HASTE HAVE I CAST AWAY ONE WHOSE LOVE FOR ME WAS PEERLESS.

SHIVA'S STATE OF MIND DID NOT ESCAPE NANDI, HIS TRUSTED SERVANT.

NOW MY MASTER WILL KNOW NO PEACE UNTIL MOTHER PARVATI RETURNS.

MEANWHILE, PARVATI HAD ALREADY REACHED THE EARTH AND LAY AS AN INFANT UNDER A PUNNAI TREE, WHERE SHE WAS FOUND BY THE CHIEF OF THE PARAVARS, A CLAN OF FISHERMEN.

WHAT A LOVELY CHILD! NO DOUBT IT IS GOD'S GIFT TO ME. I'LL CALL HER PARVATI.

LITTLE PARVATI USED TO GO WITH HER FOSTER FATHER WHENEVER HE WENT FISHING.

LOOK! A HUGE FISH!

AS SHE GREW UP, SHE EVEN LEARNT TO ROW THE BOAT.

YOU ARE A REAL HELP TO ME, PARVATI.

A PRETTY GIRL!

STRONG AND CLEVER TOO!

LUCKY IS THE MAN WHO WEDS HER!

MEANWHILE AT KAILASA —

NANDI, I CAN NO LONGER LIVE WITHOUT PARVATI!

MY LORD, WHY DON'T YOU GO DOWN TO EARTH AND CLAIM HER?

HOW CAN I, NANDI? SHE WILL NOW MARRY A FISHERMAN.

THEN I WILL SEE TO IT THAT YOU ARE FORCED TO BECOME A FISHERMAN.

ASSUMING THE FORM OF A HUGE SHARK, NANDI HEADED FOR THE COAST WHERE THE PARAVARS LIVED.

A SHARK!

QUICK! WE MUST GET IT!

BUT BEFORE THE FISHERMEN COULD ACT, THE SHARK ATTACKED...

...AND THE TWO FISHERMEN FOUND THEMSELVES IN THE WATER.

AS THE DAYS WENT BY, THE SHARK BECAME A REGULAR MENACE.

OUR NETS ARE TORN.

AND OUR BOATS IN PIECES!

WHAT SHALL WE DO?

AT LAST, THE CHIEF OF THE PARAVARS CAME UP WITH AN AWARD.

I WILL OFFER THE HAND OF MY DAUGHTER TO THE ONE WHO CAPTURES THE SHARK.

MANY A YOUNG MAN TRIED...

...AND FAILED.

THE DESPERATE PARAVARS AT LAST SOUGHT DIVINE HELP.

O COMPASSIONATE ONE, SAVE US FROM THE SHARK.

THE DAUGHTER OF THE CHIEF OF THE PARAVARS TOO PRAYED.

LORD, COME TO OUR RESCUE. DON'T FAIL US IN THE HOUR OF NEED.

SHIVA HEARD HER PRAYER.

HE APPEARED BEFORE THE CHIEF OF THE PARAVARS AS A YOUNG FISHERMAN.

I HAVE COME TO CATCH THE SHARK.

OUR TRIBE WILL BE INDEBTED TO YOU FOREVER, IF YOU SUCCEED.

NET IN HAND, SHIVA WENT DOWN INTO THE SEA.

WHEN HE CAST HIS NET, THE SHARK WHO WAS NONE OTHER THAN NANDI, SURRENDERED HIMSELF.

MY MISSION IS FULFILLED.

AS SHIVA DRAGGED THE SHARK ASHORE—

YOU ARE OUR SAVIOUR.

HOW FORTUNATE FOR ME THAT THIS BRAVE MAN HAS CAUGHT THE SHARK!

SHIVA, THE FISHERMAN, MARRIED PARVATI, THE FISHERWOMAN. NANDI ASSUMED HIS TRUE FORM AND CARRIED THE TWO TO KAILASA.

SHIVA AND MARKANDEYA

SAGE MRIKANDU OBSERVED SEVERE PENANCES TO PROPITIATE LORD SHIVA.

WHEN LORD SHIVA APPEARED BEFORE HIM—

LORD, FAVOUR ME WITH A SON.

DO YOU WANT A SON WHO WILL LIVE LONG THOUGH LACKING IN VIRTUES...

...OR A SON WHO WILL BE WISE AND VIRTUOUS BUT WILL LIVE FOR ONLY SIXTEEN YEARS?

I WILL HAVE THE VIRTUOUS SON, MY LORD.

GRANTING THE WISH OF THE SAGE, LORD SHIVA VANISHED.

IN DUE COURSE, MARUDVATI, MRIKANDU'S WIFE, GAVE BIRTH TO A SON.

THE BOY SHALL BE NAMED MARKANDEYA.

WHILE BARELY SIXTEEN, MARKANDEYA HAD MASTERED THE VEDAS.

MRIKANDU, YOU ARE FORTUNATE TO HAVE SUCH A BRILLIANT SON.

WHEN THE VISITING SAGES LEFT—

I CANNOT FORGET THAT ALL THIS BRILLIANCE WILL SOON BE PUT OUT BY CRUEL DEATH.

JUST THEN MARKANDEYA CAME HOME WITH THE FLOWERS FOR WORSHIP.

MOTHER! WHY ARE YOU WEEPING? WHAT CAN I DO TO MAKE YOU SMILE?

WHY DON'T YOU SPEAK, MOTHER? DO YOU THINK I CAN'T GET YOU WHAT YOU WANT? I AM NOT A CHILD...

...I WILL BE SIXTEEN YEARS OLD TOMORROW!

SON, THAT IS WHY YOUR MOTHER IS WEEPING.

WHY? WHAT IS WRONG WITH BEING SIXTEEN?

I WILL EXPLAIN. LISTEN!

WHEN MRIKANDU TOLD HIM ABOUT THE EVENTS LEADING TO HIS BIRTH —

DON'T CRY, MOTHER. I WILL NOT DIE.

I WILL SEEK IMMORTALITY THROUGH THE GRACE OF SHIVA WHO IS THE CONQUEROR OF DEATH.

MAY YOU SUCCEED BY HIS GRACE!

SHIVA, I LEAVE MY SON TO YOUR MERCY. PROTECT HIM.

EARLY NEXT MORNING, MARKANDEYA REACHED THE SEA-SHORE WHERE HE MADE A SHIVA LINGA OUT OF THE WET SAND...

...AND ADORNED IT WITH FLOWERS.

THEN HE SAT DOWN TO PRAY.

TOWARDS NIGHTFALL, HE BEGAN TO SING AND DANCE BEFORE THE LORD.

YAMA CAUGHT MARKANDEYA'S NECK IN THE NOOSE...

...AND DRAGGED HIM.

LORD, PROTECT ME.

THE NEXT MOMENT, SHIVA SPRANG FROM THE LINGA AND KICKED YAMA ON THE CHEST.

LORD!

LORD, PARDON ME.

WHEN YAMA DEPARTED—

O LORD, THE SOURCE OF LIFE, I SALUTE YOU.

MARKANDEYA, YOU WILL FOREVER BE FREE FROM DEATH. YOU WILL BE IMMORTAL.

SHIVA VANISHED...

...AND MARKANDEYA RETURNED HOME.

MY SON!

MOTHER! THE LORD DID SAVE ME!

GANESHA

ONE DAY, PARVATI, SHIVA'S WIFE, POSTED NANDI, HIS GANA,* AT THE DOOR TO HER PALACE.

I AM GOING TO HAVE MY BATH. DO NOT LET ANYONE ENTER AND DISTURB ME.

A LITTLE LATER, SHIVA CAME THERE. NANDI WAS IN A DILEMMA.

WHAT SHOULD I DO? HOW CAN I STOP HIM FROM ENTERING HIS OWN HOME?

* ATTENDANT.

1

SHIVA ENTERED THE PALACE AND STRODE INTO THE INNER ROOMS.

MY LORD, HERE? BUT NANDI WAS TOLD...

NANDI HAS DISOBEYED ME. YOU MAY BE MY HUSBAND BUT HE HAD NO RIGHT TO LET YOU ENTER!

HA! HA!

SHIVA WAS AMUSED BUT PARVATI WAS ANNOYED.

I MUST HAVE A GANA OF MY OWN WHO WILL OBEY ME ALONE.

SHE SPOKE TO HER FRIENDS ABOUT IT.

YOU ARE RIGHT. NONE OF THE GANAS CAN REALLY BE CALLED YOUR OWN.

WHY DON'T YOU CREATE A GANA WHO WILL OWE FIRST ALLEGIANCE TO YOU?

A GOOD SUGGESTION. I SHALL.

SHE GATHERED THE SAFFRON PASTE FROM HER OWN BODY AND CREATED A BOY.

WHEN SHE FINISHED, SHE GAZED IN ADMIRATION AT HER OWN CREATION.

HOW HANDSOME HE IS! HOW STRONG HE LOOKS!

3

SHE DECKED HIM WITH ORNAMENTS AND BLESSED HIM. THEN —

YOU ARE MY SON — MY VERY OWN SON. I HAVE NONE ELSE TO CALL MY OWN.

COMMAND ME, MOTHER. WHAT SHOULD I DO?

TAKE THIS STAFF AND FOLLOW ME.

SHE LED HIM TO THE DOOR.

STAND HERE AND LET NO ONE ENTER WITHOUT MY PERMISSION.

A LITTLE LATER —

WHO COULD THAT BOY BE? I HAVE NEVER SEEN HIM BEFORE.

4

TO SHIVA'S ASTONISHMENT, THE YOUTH BARRED HIS WAY.

HALT! NO ONE ENTERS WITHOUT MY MOTHER'S PERMISSION.

SHIVA WAS TAKEN ABACK.

FOOLISH BOY! DO YOU KNOW WHO I AM? MOVE OUT OF MY WAY.

WITHOUT UTTERING A WORD, THE YOUTH STRUCK SHIVA WITH HIS STAFF.

SHIVA WAS FURIOUS.

FOOL! I AM SHIVA, PARVATI'S HUSBAND. HOW DARE YOU FORBID ME TO ENTER MY OWN HOME!

BUT THE YOUTH ONLY RAISED HIS STAFF AND HIT SHIVA ONCE AGAIN.

SHIVA TURNED TO HIS GANAS.

WHO IS THAT FOOL? WHAT IS HE DOING THERE? THROW HIM OUT AND REPORT TO ME.

SHIVA LEFT AND THE GANAS TURNED UPON THE YOUTH.

GET AWAY WITH YOU OR YOU WILL RECEIVE A TASTE OF MY VALOUR.

YOU GET AWAY FROM HERE, IF YOU VALUE YOUR LIFE.

YOU SEEM TO FORGET THAT WE ARE SHIVA'S GANAS.

SHIVA IS MY MOTHER'S LORD. WHAT SHOULD I DO? SHOULD I FIGHT THEM OR SHOULDN'T I?

MEANWHILE, INDOORS PARVATI HAD HEARD THE COMMOTION. SHE SENT HER FRIEND OUT.

PLEASE FIND OUT WHAT THAT NOISE IS ALL ABOUT.

THE FRIEND SOON RETURNED.

THEY ARE THREATENING YOUR SON. PLEASE DON'T ALLOW THEM TO LOWER YOUR PRESTIGE.

PARVATI HESITATED FOR A MOMENT.

SHIVA IS AFTER ALL MY HUSBAND...

BUT WHY DID HE TRY TO FORCE HIS WAY IN? LET WHAT HAS TO HAPPEN, HAPPEN.

SHE SENT THE FRIEND OUT ONCE AGAIN.

TELL MY SON NOT TO GIVE IN TO **ANYONE**.

THE FRIEND CAME OUT.

GENTLE SIR, YOUR MOTHER SAYS THAT YOU SHOULD NOT LET ANYONE ENTER.

THE BOY WAS NO LONGER IN DOUBT. HE TURNED TO THE GANAS.

I AM THE SON OF PARVATI. YOU ARE THE GANAS OF SHIVA. YOU MUST CARRY OUT HIS ORDERS AND I — HERS.

I REPEAT, SHIVA SHALL NOT ENTER WITHOUT MY MOTHER'S PERMISSION.

NOW, THE GANAS WERE DOUBTFUL.

HE IS PARVATI'S SON. WHAT SHOULD WE DO? WOULD SHIVA STILL WANT US TO THROW HIM OUT?

THEY REPORTED TO SHIVA.

LORD, IT IS PARVATI'S **OWN** SON WHO REFUSES TO LET YOU IN.

ALAS, PARVATI! YOU HAVE GONE TOO FAR. YOU HAVE LEFT ME WITH NO ALTERNATIVE.

9

SO THE GANAS, FULLY ARRAYED FOR WAR, WENT BACK TO THE BOY. HE WAS AMUSED WHEN HE SAW THEM.

I, A MERE BOY CARRYING OUT MY MOTHER'S ORDERS, WELCOME YOU, THE LEADERS OF SHIVA'S HORDES.

THE GANAS RUSHED AT HIM.

NANDI GRABBED HIS LEGS.

BUT—

HA! THAT'S BETTER.

AA...A.AH!

11

MANY OF THE GANAS FELL.

THE REST FLED AS FAST AS THEY COULD.

THE BOY ONCE AGAIN TOOK HIS POST AT THE DOOR.

MEANWHILE, WHEN BRAHMA, VISHNU AND INDRA HEARD THE UPROAR, THEY TALKED THE MATTER OVER WITH SAGE NARADA.

GO TO LORD SHIVA. HE MAY NEED YOU.

THEY WENT ACCORDINGLY AND BOWED BEFORE SHIVA.

LORD, WE ARE HERE TO DO YOUR BIDDING.

SHIVA TOLD THEM ALL.

...AND HE DARES TO PREVENT ME FROM ENTERING MY OWN HOME.

O BRAHMA, GO THERE AND TRY TO BRING HIM UNDER CONTROL.

I SHALL GO DISGUISED AS A BRAHMAN.

ACCOMPANIED BY MANY SAGES, BRAHMA LEFT ON HIS MISSION.

14

AS THEY NEARED HIM, THE YOUTH SUDDENLY JUMPED FORWARD AND —

THAT SHOULD TEACH YOU A LESSON.

BRAHMA WAS TAKEN UNAWARES.

I HAVE NOT COME TO FIGHT. I HAVE COME TO MAKE PEACE. LISTEN TO ME!

FOR AN ANSWER, THE YOUTH LIFTED HIS CLUB MENACINGLY.

THE DEVAS, LED BY INDRA, AND THE GANAS, BY KARTIKEYA, FELL UPON THE BOY FROM ALL DIRECTIONS.

BUT THE BOY FACED THEM VALIANTLY.

MEANWHILE, PARVATI LEARNED OF ALL THAT HAD HAPPENED; SHE WAS FURIOUS.

HOW DARE THEY HARASS MY SON!

THEN AND THERE SHE CREATED THE TWO SHAKTIS, KALI AND DURGA.

GO! ASSIST MY SON.

KALI STOOD BETWEEN THE BOY AND THE ENEMY. OPENING HER MOUTH WIDE, SHE SWALLOWED THEIR WEAPONS...

...AND HURLED THEM BACK.

DURGA TOOK THE FORM OF LIGHTNING...

...AND DESTROYED THE ENEMIES' WEAPONS BEFORE THEY COULD REACH THE BOY.

BETWEEN THE TWO OF THEM THEY DID NOT LET A SINGLE WEAPON COME ANYWHERE NEAR THE BOY'S SWINGING CLUB.

INDRA AND HIS DEVAS WERE COMPLETELY ROUTED.

EVEN KARTIKEYA, WHO HAD KILLED THE INVINCIBLE TARAKASURA, WAS HELPLESS.

THEY HELD COUNCIL.

WHAT SHOULD WE DO?

LET US GO BACK TO SHIVA.

O LORD, WE HAVE SEEN AND HEARD OF MANY BATTLES BUT NEVER HAVE WE SEEN OR HEARD OF SUCH A WARRIOR!

THEIR PRAISE ONLY INFURIATED SHIVA.

I WILL HAVE TO KILL HIM WITH MY OWN HANDS.

SHIVA THUNDERED OUT FOLLOWED BY ALL OF THEM.

UNPERTURBED BY THE SIGHT OF SHIVA, THE BOY ATTACKED! ALL THE CHIEF GODS. ONE BY ONE THEY FELL.

AS SHIVA WATCHED HIM FIGHT, HE WAS AMAZED.

HE IS INVINCIBLE. HE CAN ONLY BE KILLED BY CUNNING. I MUST WATCH FOR AN OPPORTUNITY.

THE SAME THOUGHT HAD STRUCK VISHNU TOO. HE SPOKE TO SHIVA.

I SHALL USE MY POWERS OF DELUSION TO FIGHT HIM, IF YOU PER- MIT ME.

YOU MAY. THAT IS THE ONLY WAY.

BUT KALI AND DURGA DIVINED THEIR INTENTIONS.

WHAT SHOULD WE DO?

LET US CONFER ALL OUR STRENGTH ON THE YOUTH. !THEN EVEN VISHNU'S MAYA WILL PROVE INEFFECTUAL.

WITH THE ADDED STRENGTH OF THE TWO SHAKTIS, THE BOY SWUNG HIS CLUB AT VISHNU.

VISHNU HAD TO USE ALL HIS ENERGY TO DODGE IT.

SHIVA SAW HIS PLIGHT AND CHARGED WITH HIS TRIDENT.

23

BUT—

SHIVA TOOK UP HIS BOW.

THE BOY DASHED IT TO THE GROUND WITH HIS CLUB.

NO WONDER MY GANAS WERE HELPLESS.

THE NEXT MOMENT—

HE'S BACK.

THE BOY LIFTED HIS CLUB...

...BUT IT WAS CUT IN TWO BY VISHNU'S DISCUS.

THE BOY HURLED THE PIECE THAT WAS LEFT IN HIS HAND...

... BUT VISHNU'S MOUNT, GARUDA, CAUGHT IT AND PROTECTED HIS MASTER.

THEN, AS THE BOY PICKED UP HIS STAFF TO HIT VISHNU, SHIVA CAME UP FROM BEHIND AND...

...CUT OFF HIS HEAD.

FOR A MOMENT ALL ON THE SCENE STOOD STILL, THEIR GAZE FIXED ON THE VALIANT HERO.

THEN THE DEVAS AND THE GANAS BECAME JUBILANT.

BUT SHIVA WAS TROUBLED.

ALAS! WHAT HAVE I DONE? HOW SHALL I FACE PARVATI? HE WAS CREATED BY HER. THAT MADE HIM MY SON TOO.

MEANWHILE, WHEN PARVATI LEARNT OF HER SON'S DEATH —

MY SON WAS KILLED BY UNFAIR MEANS. FOR THIS THE DEVAS AND GANAS SHALL ALL DIE.

28

THEY PROPITIATED PARVATI AND PLEADED FOR MERCY.

O GREAT GODDESS, HAVE MERCY ON US. WE SHALL ACCOMPLISH WHATEVER YOU ASK OF US. FORGIVE US.

I WILL. BUT MY SON MUST REGAIN HIS LIFE AND MUST HAVE AN HONOURABLE STATUS AMONG YOU.

THEY WENT TO SHIVA AND PUT PARVATI'S CONDITIONS BEFORE HIM.

IT SHALL BE DONE. FOR THE SAKE OF PEACE AND HAPPINESS.

GO NORTH. BRING THE HEAD OF THE FIRST CREATURE THAT CROSSES YOUR PATH. FIT THAT HEAD TO THE BOY'S BODY AND IT WILL COME TO LIFE.

IT WAS A SINGLE-TUSKED ELEPHANT THAT MET THEM.

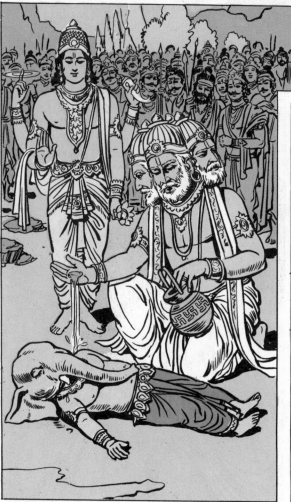

THEY BROUGHT THE HEAD BACK AND FITTED IT TO THE BODY OF THE BOY.

THE BOY SAT UP.

DELIGHTED, THEY SHOWED HIM TO PARVATI. BUT SHE WAS ONLY PARTIALLY APPEASED.

WHAT ABOUT HIS STATUS?

AT THAT MOMENT INDRA AND THE OTHER GODS LED SHIVA TO HER.

SHIVA BOWED BEFORE PARVATI.

FORGIVE ME, PARVATI. ARROGANCE IS CHARACTERISTIC OF THE MALE. THIS VALIANT YOUTH SHALL BE ANOTHER SON OF MINE.

THEN SHIVA PLACED HIS HAND ON THE BOY'S HEAD.

EVEN AS A MERE BOY YOU SHOWED GREAT VALOUR. YOU SHALL BE GANESHA, THE PRESIDING OFFICER OF ALL MY GANAS. YOU SHALL BE WORTHY OF WORSHIP FOREVER. YOU SHALL ALSO BE CALLED VIGHNESHWARA, THE QUELLER OF OBSTACLES.

SHIVA AND PARVATI ONCE AGAIN BEGAN TO LIVE HAPPILY IN THEIR ABODE AT MOUNT KAILAS, DELIGHTED BY THE PRESENCE OF THEIR TWO SONS. TO THIS DAY, BEFORE ANY VENTURE IS UNDERTAKEN, IT IS GANESHA WHO IS INVOKED AND WHOSE BLESSINGS ARE SOUGHT.

KARTTIKEYA

IN ANCIENT TIMES, THE DEVAS AND THE ASURAS WERE FOREVER AT WAR AND OFTEN IT WAS THE ASURAS WHO WERE DEFEATED.

AFTER ONE CRUSHING DEFEAT, AN ASURA KING NAMED AKHIRSEN WENT TO HIS DAUGHTER, MAYA, A SORCERESS.

THE DEVAS ARE VICTORIOUS AGAIN. O THE SHAME OF IT!

DON'T WORRY, FATHER. I WILL NOT REST TILL I TEACH THE DEVAS A LESSON!

TAKING THE FORM OF A BEAUTIFUL WOMAN MAYA WENT TO THE FOREST WHERE THE GREAT SAGE KASHYAPA SAT DEEP IN MEDITATION.

I WILL MARRY THIS SAGE AND BRING FORTH CHILDREN MORE POWERFUL THAN THE DEVAS.

HER MAGIC CHANGED THE PLACE INTO A PRETTY GARDEN WHERE SHE DANCED AND SANG MELODIOUSLY...

...TILL THE SAGE LOOKED UP.

PLEASE LET ME SERVE YOU AS YOUR WIFE, O HOLY ONE.

HOW CAN I REFUSE YOU, NOBLE MAIDEN!

SAGE KASHYAPA AND THE ASURA PRINCESS LIVED HAPPILY IN THE FOREST. IN DUE COURSE A SON WAS BORN TO THEM.

YOU, MY MIGHTY SURAPADMAN, SHALL BE THE LORD OF THE THREE WORLDS.

LATER MAYA GAVE BIRTH TO TWO MORE SONS WHOM SHE NAMED SIMHAMUKHA AND TARAKA.

I CAN'T WAIT FOR THE DAY WHEN YOU WILL CONQUER THE DEVAS AND MAKE THEM OUR SLAVES.

THE VIRTUOUS SAGE OF COURSE WAS IGNORANT OF MAYA'S DESIGNS.

SO WHEN THE BOYS CAME OF AGE—

I AM GOING AWAY, MY SONS. TAKE CARE OF YOUR MOTHER, LEAD A VIRTUOUS LIFE AND BE DEVOTED TO THE LORD.

NOW IS THE TIME TO ACT. PROPITIATE LORD SHIVA AND OBTAIN BOONS WHICH WILL MAKE YOU INVINCIBLE.

AS YOU WISH, MOTHER.

THE THREE LEFT HOME AND PERFORMED SEVERE PENANCES TO WIN THE GRACE OF SHIVA.

BUT THEIR EFFORTS DID NOT BEAR FRUIT. SO SURAPADMAN, THE ELDEST, JUMPED INTO THE SACRIFICIAL FIRE.

BUT THE NEXT MOMENT HE WAS SAVED FROM ITS FLAMES BY SHIVA HIMSELF.

WHY ARE YOU SACRIFICING YOURSELF?

LORD, I WANT TO BE THE MASTER OF THE UNIVERSE. I WANT TO HAVE A BODY THAT WILL NOT PERISH.

NO ONE CAN HAVE AN IMMORTAL BODY. BUT YOU WILL BE INVINCIBLE AND RULE THE UNIVERSE FOR A LONG TIME TO COME.

YOU SHALL NOT BE DEFEATED BY ANY POWER EXCEPT MINE.

INTOXICATED WITH TRIUMPH, THE THREE BROTHERS RETURNED HOME AND TOLD THEIR MOTHER ABOUT SHIVA'S BOON.

AT LAST MY DREAM WILL COME TRUE.

YES, WE DON'T HAVE TO FEAR ANYONE. WE'LL SOON DRIVE THE DEVAS OUT OF HEAVEN.

THEN, RAVAGING KINGDOM AFTER KINGDOM ON THEIR ROUTE...

...THEY CAME TO DEVALOKA. THERE, IN THE FIERCE BATTLE THAT FOLLOWED, THE DEVAS WERE ROUTED...

...AND TAKEN CAPTIVE.

LATER—

HA! HA! HOW DOES IT FEEL TO BE IN BONDAGE, O INDRA, KING OF THE DEVAS?

IS THAT VAYU? HOW DEFLATED HE LOOKS!

WHAT SHOULD WE DO WITH THEM, BROTHER?

WE'LL MAKE THEM OUR SLAVES. INDRA WILL BE OUR FISHERMAN, AND VAYU OUR SWEEPER. AND...

...SURYA WILL MAKE A FINE BALL FOR OUR CHILDREN.

A BRILLIANT IDEA! HAHAHA!

SURAPADMAN HAD A MAGNIFICENT CITY BUILT BY VISHWAKARMA, THE ARCHITECT OF THE DEVAS. HE CALLED IT MAHENDRAPURI AND MADE IT HIS CAPITAL.

THE DEVAS MEANWHILE WERE LAMENTING THEIR FATE.

THEY HAVE IMPRISONED EVEN THE VALIANT JAYANTA*! WHAT SHALL WE DO?

HOW LONG CAN WE SUFFER THIS HUMILIATION?

SHIVA HAD PROMISED TO HELP US.

THAT WAS LONG AGO.

* INDRA'S SON

6

LET'S GO TO KAILAS ONCE MORE AND PRAY TO HIM.

HAVE YOU FORGOTTEN WHAT HAPPENED TO KAMA WHEN WE LAST VISITED KAILAS?

KAMA, THE GOD OF LOVE, HAD BEEN BURNT TO ASHES WHEN HE HAD TRIED TO DISTURB SHIVA'S PENANCE. LATER, HOWEVER, HE WAS RESTORED TO LIFE.

SHIVA, HAPPILY MARRIED TO PARVATI NOW, IS MORE COMPASSIONATE AND WILL SURELY LISTEN TO OUR PRAYER.

YES. LET'S GO TO KAILAS ONCE MORE.

AT KAILAS—

LORD, DRUNK WITH POWER THE MEAN ASURAS HAVE MADE US THEIR SLAVES. MY SON, JAYANTA IS THEIR PRISONER!

BE PATIENT! YOUR MISERIES WILL SOON END BECAUSE THEIR DAYS ARE NUMBERED.

7

THEN SHIVA ASSUMED A FORM WITH SIX FACES...

...FROM WHICH SIX DIVINE SPARKS SHOT FORTH...

...DAZZLING THE DEVAS WITH THEIR SPLENDOUR.

THE CHILD BORN OUT OF THESE SPARKS WILL SLAY THE ASURAS.

SHIVA THEN ASSUMED HIS ORIGINAL FORM.

VAYU, YOU AND AGNI CARRY THESE SPARKS TO GANGA. SHE'LL CARRY THEM TO THE SHARAVANA* ON THE UDAYA MOUNTAIN.

*FOREST OF REEDS

8

AGNI AND VAYU FLEW WITH THE SPARKS...

... TO GANGA.

SHIVA HAS ASKED YOU TO CARRY THESE TO THE REED FOREST ON THE UDAYA MOUNTAIN.

AS SOON AS GANGA BROUGHT THEM INTO THE SHARAVANA...

... THE SPARKS TURNED INTO SIX BABIES!

JUST THEN SIX CELESTIAL NYMPHS CALLED THE KRITTIKAS HAPPENED TO PASS BY.

NEWBORN BABIES! SIX OF THEM!

ONE FOR EACH OF US!

AND THE KRITTIKAS BEGAN TO CUDDLE THE INFANTS.

THE DEVAS CAME ON THE SCENE A LITTLE LATER.

LOOK! THE CHILD...

YOU MEAN CHILDREN!

AND THEN CAME SHIVA AND PARVATI.

SHIVA'S CHILDREN! MY CHILDREN!

AS PARVATI STEPPED CLOSER, THE BABIES MERGED INTO ONE.

MY SON!

HE IS MY SON. I HELD THE SPARKS.

NO, AGNI. HE IS MINE. I BROUGHT THEM TO THIS FOREST.

MY FOREST, O GANGA. HE WAS BORN IN MY FOREST OF REEDS. HE IS MY SON.

BUT WE ARE THE ONES WHO NURSED HIM, O GODDESS OF THE FOREST. HE IS OUR SON.

PEACE! PEACE! AS PARVATI'S SON HE WILL BE NAMED SKANDA AND AS THE SON OF THE GODDESS OF THE FOREST, SHARAVANA; AS THE KRITTIKAS' SON, KARTTIKEYA AND AS GANGA'S KUMARA; AS AGNI'S SON, MAHASENA AND AS MINE, GUHA.

HOW WILL I FONDLE A BABY WITH SIX HEADS?

THE NEXT MINUTE—

MY SON!

KARTTIKEYA WAS NOW LIKE ANY OTHER CHILD.

SOON, NINE DIVINE BEINGS EMERGED FROM THE LAKE.

THOSE ARE YOUR GANAS— VEERABAHU AND HIS COMPANIONS.

THEN, AFTER THE DEVAS HAD WORSHIPPED LORD KARTTIKEYA...

...SHIVA TOOK HIM TO HIS OWN ABODE, AT MOUNT KAILASA.

ONE DAY AT KAILASA—

PARVATI, THE TIME HAS COME FOR KARTTIKEYA TO SUBDUE TARAKASURA, SIMHAMUKHA, AND SURAPADMAN.

BUT HE IS JUST A CHILD, MY LORD, AND THEY ARE MIGHTY WARRIORS.

YES, BUT HE IS THE CHILD WITH THE DIVINE SPARK. BESIDES, HIS GANAS WILL GO WITH HIM.

SHIVA SUMMONED KARTTIKEYA AND VEERABAHU.

GET READY TO ATTACK SURAPADMAN AND HIS BROTHERS.

WHEN THE PREPARATIONS WERE COMPLETED—

YOU SHALL LEAD THE DEVAS TO VICTORY. CRUSH THE ASURAS AND LIBERATE THE DEVAS. HERE IS THE MATCHLESS VEL, YOUR SPEAR. MAY SUCCESS BE YOURS!

ARMED WITH THE SPEAR, KARTTIKEYA SET OUT IN PURSUIT OF THE ASURAS.

AFTER HE HAD COVERED SOME DISTANCE —

YOU WILL HAVE TO FACE ME, YOUNG BOY, BEFORE YOU PROCEED FURTHER.

IT WAS THE ASURA, KRAUNCHA IN THE FORM OF A MOUNTAIN.

WITHOUT A WORD, KARTTIKEYA HURLED HIS SPEAR···

···AND KRAUNCHA WAS NO MORE.

14

WHEN THE NEWS REACHED TARAKA—

KRAUNCHA DESTROYED? BY A SLIP OF A BOY?

WELL, WELL, LET ME GO AND SIZE HIM UP.

WHEN HE CAME FACE TO FACE WITH KARTTIKEYA—

DON'T MISUSE THE WEAPONS GRANTED TO YOU. RELEASE THE DEVAS. YOU AND YOUR BROTHERS WILL BE FORGIVEN.

HOW DARE YOU, YOU IMPUDENT BOY! GET AWAY...

...BEFORE I KILL YOU!

VICTORY TO SHIVA!

THIS WEAPON— THE WEAPON GIVEN TO ME BY SHIVA— CANNOT FAIL!

YOU HAVE EXHAUSTED ALL THOSE WEAPONS, TARAKA. NOW LET ME TRY THE ONE I HAVE.

KARTTIKEYA'S SPEAR FOUND ITS MARK.

TARAKASURA IS SLAIN!

VICTORY TO KARTTIKEYA!

LATER—

VEERABAHU, TARAKASURA'S DEATH MAY HAVE BROUGHT HIS BROTHERS TO THEIR SENSES. GO AS MY ENVOY TO SURAPADMAN AND ASK HIM TO STOP PERSECUTING THE DEVAS.

AS YOU COMMAND, MY LORD.

WHEN VEERABAHU REACHED SURAPADMAN'S CAPITAL, MAHENDRAPURI—

BEFORE I GO TO SURAPADMAN, I MUST SEE JAYANTA.

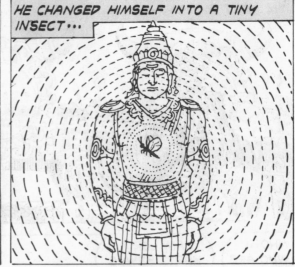

HE CHANGED HIMSELF INTO A TINY INSECT···

···AND FLEW INTO THE CITY.

IN THE PRISON—

JAYANTA, TARAKASURA IS DEAD. LORD KARTTIKEYA WILL SOON RESCUE YOU.

THEN HE FLEW INTO SURAPADMAN'S COURT.

I WILL ASSUME MY OWN FORM NOW. WILL SURAPADMAN OFFER ME A SEAT?

THE NEXT MOMENT—

A THRONE FOR ME! IT MUST BE THE WORK OF LORD KARTTIKEYA!

WHO... WHO ARE YOU?

I AM LORD KARTTIKEYA'S MESSENGER.

KARTTIKEYA! THE BOY WHO SLEW MY BROTHER!

REMEMBER KRAUNCHA... TARAKA... WHY DON'T WE RELEASE...

SIMHAMUKHA!

COWARD! NOT ANOTHER WORD!

BROTHER, IT IS UNFORTUNATE THAT WISDOM IS OFTEN MISTAKEN FOR COWARDICE.

BY SPEAKING OUT, I HAVE DONE MY DUTY. NOW IT IS FOR YOU TO TAKE THE DECISION. I WILL GO BY IT.

IT'S WAR AGAINST THAT IMPUDENT BOY.

MEANWHILE VEERABAHU HAD REACHED KARTTIKEYA'S CAMP.

IT'S NO USE. SURAPADMAN WANTED TO CAPTURE ME TOO!

WELL, WE'LL MEET THEM IN BATTLE. PREPARE TO MARCH TO MAHENDRAPURI.

WHEN KARTTIKEYA'S ARMY REACHED THE OUTSKIRTS OF MAHENDRAPURI, SURAPADMAN SENT HIS SON BANUKOPAN TO SUBDUE THEM.

BANUKOPAN FELL UPON THE DEVA ARMY.

ON THE SECOND DAY OF THE BATTLE—

COME, BANUKOPAN. TODAY, YOU SHALL NOT RETURN HOME.

I CERTAINLY WON'T. NOT TILL I'VE KILLED EVERY ONE OF YOU.

VEERABAHU RUSHED AT HIM AND THE TWO FOUGHT LONG AND HARD.

AT LAST BANUKOPAN FELL AND THE ASURAS FLED IN PANIC.

THE DEATH OF BANUKOPAN SHOOK SURAPADMAN.

SAVE US, SIMHAMUKHA!

I WILL DO MY BEST, BROTHER.

SO THE NEXT DAY SIMHAMUKHA LED THE ATTACK. THE ARMY OF THE DEVAS REELED UNDER HIS ONSLAUGHT.

THEN SIMHAMUKHA SENT A MISSILE···

···WHICH WOUND ITSELF AROUND VEERABAHU, HIS BROTHER AND THE REST OF THE ARMY···

···AND HURLED THEM···

···FAR, FAR AWAY FROM THE BATTLEFIELD.

BUT KARTTIKEYA MEANWHILE HAD SENT FORTH SEVERAL MISSILES TO COUNTER THE MOVE.

SOON—

THEN KARTTIKEYA TURNED HIS ATTENTION TO SIMHAMUKHA.

YOU SHOULD NOT MISUSE THE POWERS ACQUIRED BY YOU. YOU SHOULD...

HAVE YOU COME HERE TO FIGHT OR TO PREACH?

AFTER A FIERCE BATTLE KARTTIKEYA HURLED INDRAYUDHA* AT SIMHAMUKHA.

AS SIMHAMUKHA FELL—

YOUR WEAPON HAS SHATTERED MY EGO. NOW I SEE YOU IN ALL YOUR GLORY. O LORD, BLESS ME.

THE MERCIFUL KARTTIKEYA BLESSED SIMHAMUKHA.

YOU SHALL SERVE GODDESS KALI AS HER VEHICLE.

*INDRA'S WEAPON, THE THUNDERBOLT

24

THE NEXT DAY SURAPADMAN HIMSELF LED THE ASURAS TO THE BATTLEFIELD.

WE MUST DEFEAT KARTTIKEYA! SHOW YOUR METTLE TODAY.

WHEN HE CAME FACE TO FACE WITH KARTTIKEYA—

MERCY OR DOOM? CHOOSE!

IMPUDENT CHILD! I HAVE COME TO SILENCE YOU ONCE AND FOR ALL.

THE TWO FOES MET.

THIS BOY IS NOT AS RAW AS I HAD EXPECTED! WHY, HE FIGHTS LIKE A SEASONED WARRIOR!

I'LL HAVE TO RESORT TO SORCERY. THAT'S THE ONLY WAY TO QUELL HIM!

THE NEXT MOMENT—

WH...WHAT IS THIS! MY CHARIOT IS MOVING TOWARDS THAT BOY.

SOON—

I MUST THANK YOU, SURAPADMAN, FOR PROVIDING ME WITH AN EXCELLENT CHARIOT.

I'LL CHANGE MY FORM AND ATTACK HIM.

SURAPADMAN QUICKLY ASSUMED THE FORM OF A HUGE BIRD...

...AND CHARGED AT KARTTIKEYA.

KARTTIKEYA HOWEVER USING INDRA IN THE FORM OF PEACOCK AS HIS MOUNT...

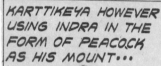

BUT SURAPADMAN ESCAPED IN THE NICK OF TIME BY TAKING THE FORM OF A TREE.

...LASHED OUT AT HIM.

LEARN, O BLIND ONE! DARKNESS CANNOT HIDE BEFORE LIGHT!

AS THE SPEAR CUT THE TREE IN TWO, SURAPADMAN EMERGED UNSCATHED IN HIS NATURAL FORM.

I'LL CRUSH HIM WITH MY BULK!

SURAPADMAN CHARGED TOWARDS KARTTIKEYA.

I'LL CRUSH YOU UNDERFOOT. AND THAT WILL BE THE END OF YOU.

QUICK AS LIGHTNING, KARTTIKEYA HURLED HIS SPEAR AT HIM.

AND —

A-A-H

AS HE FELL, A GREAT CHANGE CAME OVER SURAPADMAN.

LORD, PARDON ME. I REPENT FOR MY EVIL ACTS. LORD, I SEEK REFUGE IN YOU.

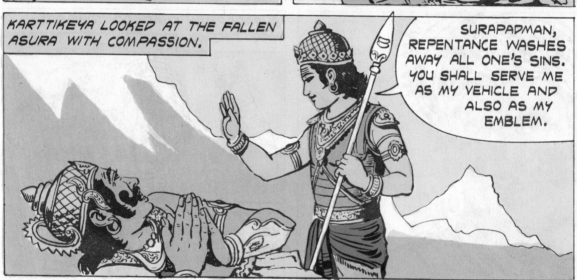

KARTTIKEYA LOOKED AT THE FALLEN ASURA WITH COMPASSION.

SURAPADMAN, REPENTANCE WASHES AWAY ALL ONE'S SINS. YOU SHALL SERVE ME AS MY VEHICLE AND ALSO AS MY EMBLEM.

THUS SURAPADMAN ASSUMED TWO FORMS — ONE OF A PEACOCK TO SERVE AS A VEHICLE TO THE LORD AND ANOTHER OF A COCK TO ADORN KARTTIKEYA'S FLAG POST.

O KARTTIKEYA, WE BOW TO YOU IN REVERENCE.

Timeless Treasures

The legendary sagas of Amar Chitra Katha are now
available as 5-in-1 digests with a distinctive compilation
of five enthralling tales in one comic book.

Stories of Birbal	Great Rulers of India
Stories from the Jatakas	Brave Rajputs
Stories from the Panchatantra	Ancient Tales of Wit and Wisdom
Stories of Rama	Further Stories from the Jatakas
More Stories from the Jatakas	Stories from the Bhagawat
Devotees of Vishnu	Stories of Buddha
Heroes from the Mahabharata	Stories from the Mahabharata
Stories from Sanskrit Drama	Great Freedom Fighters

**Each 160-page digest is now available at a special online price of
Rs 175 (MRP Rs 195) at www.AmarChitraKatha.com. Start your collection today!**

INDIA BOOK HOUSE
Mahalaxmi Chambers, 5th Floor, 22 Bhulabhai Desai Road, Mumbai 400 026, India.
Tel.: 2352 3409, 2352 5636 Fax: 2353 8406 E-mail: info@amarchitrakath.com